The Old Testament

Sir Frank Dody, the Poet

To order additional copies of this book, contact:
Xlibris
844-714-8691
www.Xlibris.com
Orders@Xlibris.com

ISBN: Softcover   978-1-6641-3875-9
        EBook   978-1-6641-3876-6

Print information available on the last page

Rev. date: 10/30/2020

הנשיה תירבה

Fervent Devotion

The Old Testament is dedicated to
everyone that has found themselves at the finish line
only to find out that it is actually the starting point of another race.

"Ending is often only a new beginning."
- One/G\

Contents

# Death Certificate

Proem Genesis
Sir Frank Dody,
this one's from the heart.

Bridge
What are you doing?
I made a hundred (thousand),
and then I went through it. If you're
talking money then I speak it fluently.
I walk it,
I talk it,
I live it,
I do it.
Yes.

Panorama
I came from the bottom, I put that on all of my partners.
I told them don't worry, I've got them.
She wanted Red Bottoms. I told her, "come and give me some knowledge,"
and then I took her out to Foley's.
I overdosed, then I quit smack.
The trunk's in the front, and the brain's in the back.
"They tried to throw me away, do you feel me?
I woke up with her hand on my head praying."
Do YOU hear me?

My grandmother prayed.
I love YOU for that.

Pan. III
I bought a K, but don't make it (onomatopoeic interjection).
I've got a page, I'm looking for stats (statistics).
A Red Lobster dinner, I bought it for Mack.
I'm on the curb, come and run into that;
if it's a problem I'm gripping the (onomatopoeic reoccurrence).
Back in the cage, I did it for Dooley.
I caught a play and I didn't have a ruler.
I'm on the page, I think it's amusing.
If it gets off the line, then I'm running through it.

You already know what it is, do you hear me? What
do they know about sacrifices? You already know what
it is. I've sacrificed for real and lost a lot; lost everything.
That's One right there; when God talks you better close your mouth
"[I] did this on myself," do you feel me?" Yes, you know what it is.
Don't even worry about it, I'm on it.

Apogee
Before we begin, I'd like to say this about Sir Frank Dody –
I enjoy the new sound.

✡

Proem Genesis
I murdered the bag; yes, I made a killing.
I'll cut off your hands if you're thinking about stealing.
"A bust-down Rolex, [I have] no time for it.
My girl likes Prada, I like Tom Ford."

Bridge
I'm back in my bag. I'm back in my bag
I'm making them mad; I'm not popping tags,
I'm stacking my cash. I'm back in my bag.
I'm back in my bag. My shorty looks bad;
I'm gwoping the stash; I'm doing the dash.

Panorama
Her (my girlfriend's) English is bad, I can barely understand.
I had to find a new plug in Japan.
We never spoke, but I cash-apped him some bands (thousands).
As a matter of fact, I got a hundred (thousand) in my hand right now.

With vanilla extract, I'm whipping the box.
We never front, we get it off the top.
I feel like Shaq, I'm over the block.
I feel like a chef, I'm over the pot.

Pan. III
A bust-down Rolex, but I don't have time for it.
My girl likes Prada, I like Tom Ford.
I've got 4 cars
got one crib,
but I want another.
What do you think I'm on the grind for?
My hustle is relentless.
I stayed on my pivot.
I couldn't be lazy, I had to go get it.

My girl washed the dishes.
I'm focused on digits.
They broke in my crib and
they ran through the kitchen.
I'm clutching that Smith & (Wesson)
Elijah Muhammad, as God as my witness –

"I won't leave a witness."
Pan. V
I'm working that pistol.
I did like fitness.
If you (Lucifer) get hit
I bet you flip like a gymnast.
If loyalty is not it then
what are you building?
I murdered the bag;
yes, I made a killing.
I'll cut off your hands
if you're thinking about stealing.
"Jesus Christ, I studied the Scripture."

I bought a (onomatopoeic interjection),
then got a (onomatopoeic reoccurrence).
I'm weighing the (onomatopoeic reoccurrence),
then sold it two.
Pan. VII

When she came through
I gave her the (onomatopoeic reoccurrence).
When we'd gotten through.
I told her to shoo.
"Hey, hold on, hold on, hold on, hold on, hold on!
Let it breathe."

Apogee
"Frank, what's this about?
I kind of understand,
but then again
I don't understand.
Do you get what I'm saying?"

Zenith / Act I
"Baby, stop laughing –
like do you even understand me
when I talk?"

♔ *Confirmation*

Proem Genesis
What's good with you?
This is your boy Sir Frank Dody,
and the way that I thought that we were rocking was
what's already understood doesn't have to be explained.
Do you hear me?
At least that's what I thought.

Bridge
"Ice game, get the flu with the bust-down.
A hundred bands all blues tell me what now?
Vvs's, chain heavy with the bling blaow (onomatopoeic interjection).
Skert skert (onomatopoeic interjection), in the coupe with the top down."
Understand, Girl, you know that I love you.
Understand, Girl, you know that I want you.
Understand, Girl, you know that I've got you.
But, there are just things that I can't do.

Panorama
"Blue bag, blue face, blue hundreds;
get a new coupe. I cop a new coupe every summer.
I might dump hard. I might stunt hard. Watch me run it.
I'm a big dog. I've got them pissed off to their stomachs.

I don't play; I just get a check. I just run it up.
She wants that D. I'll put it in her guts and tear her stomach up.
I don't buy much, I just keep stacking commas up.
I'm hitting it from the back. Baby said, "Stop that's enough."

Pan. III
I quit smoking years ago, now I only drink.
This diamond-studded bezel's got the Rolex leaking like a sink.
She sucked it with her eyes open. I swear to God she didn't blink.
Then she asked, "Do you love me?"
I responded, "What do you think?

Girl, I want you – and you know.
But, there are things that I can't do.
And, there are things that I won't do.
But, understand Girl, I've got you.

Apogee
You know I've got you, Baby.
That's one hundred.
That's on my name,
Frank Dody (onomatopoeic interjection).

 *D4L*

Proem Genesis
All I've ever needed…
Girl, you already know…
"Do you want something like that?
All right, I'm with it"

Bridge
All I ever really wanted was a rider.
I've been out here hustling and looking for a rider.
Girl, you already know I want a rider.
I'm just out here until I get me a rider.

I need a rider.
I want a rider.
I found a rider.
I jumped inside her.

Panorama
I don't play that disrespect,
I'm a gangster, Girl, I'm sorry.
I don't like to go to clubs,
I don't like to go to parties.
I'm an introvert,
all I do is work,
and get a check or something.
I'm in that Benz
chaffering a ten (beautiful woman)
getting some neck or something.

If I go in, I do not pretend.
"Bring the tech or something
She's a thick one
and she wants to kick it – David Beckham or something.
I'm in the kitchen, Girl, I've got the recipe.
It's no limit to this pimping – call me Master P.
Drinking Coors Light back to back on top of the balcony
one night, I gave her that drunk D and now she's after me.

Pan. III
Yes, I've got you, Baby.
Yes, I've got you, Girl.
If I put this in your life then I could change your world.
Yes.

You asked me what I needed or you know what I wanted in a woman.
I mean basically, that's it,
I just need a rider.

Pan. V
A loud noise from the distance traveled to where I was standing,
Ever so excruciating,
Ever so doubtful,
Ever so continuous.

The noise spoke to me.
I listened, not to hear, but to see.

Pan. VII
I could see the pain wedged in its lurid voice.
I could see that it was left with no other choice.
I could see the weight of carrying such remorse.

When the noise finally passed me by,
and I turned to see it walk away as
most men do when admiring the
shape of a women's body, I
saw nothing, I saw no
one, I saw only the
ever lingering
shadows of
darkness.

Proem Genesis

Love is complex to most although it doesn't really have to be.
Without you, by my side at night while sleeping I often feel the devil after me.
Though pain sometimes repeats itself, it is not finite – as is a casualty.
But what we fall victim to time and time again is focusing
more on the artist instead of the masterpiece.

You asked me what I needed and I told you – yet you did not fulfill that need.
You asked me to show you where my wounds were, and I did –
yet you allowed them to continue to bleed.
I protested with you that no one was perfect, and to that fact,
you and I both were great examples indeed.
But when it was time to disperse blame equally, instead of
accepting what was yours you'd rather leave.

Roses are red,
violets are blue,
and now i am with you.

Bridge

We made plans for the future but they fell through.
You walked all over my heart although I loved you.
Disappointed with myself. Why did I trust you?
Girl look at everything I did for you.
Look what I did for you.
You know what I did for you.
Just check what I did for you.
I can't believe I love you.

Panorama

Chalk them out and watch me whip a whole eighth down.
When other people left your side Girl I stayed down.
They brought that pressure to your M, I brought that K out.
"Chopper with a pole, crib looks like a safe house."
I was packed in on the backend; I had a Mack 10.
Metal detector – sneak the strap in.
Girl, I loved you and you knew that.
I gave you my trust too, you ran through that.
I tried to scuff you.
You told me cuff you.
I told you to slow it down,

I'm not trying to rush you.
I was feeling you – scratch that I was into you.
They say love's a drug, I just pray it's not medicinal.
It's the strongest thing that I've felt yet.
I just pray you don't forget what goes around comes back.
I was focused on the money, you thought I was off track.
All the love that I was giving I pray it was paid back.
They say love is a gamble. I felt it was worth it.
But Nobody's perfect. How could I not've earned that?
How could I not earn that?

Apogee / Act II

Frank, I just don't know how to say this.
But I can't. I just can't do this anymore. You told me what you wanted
and I told you that I got you.
I told you I can be everything that you need.
But, Frank I can't.
You never have time for me. You always recording, you're always working,
and I understand that. I understand all of that.
I know you want to be a provider, but I need you – I need all of you.
And, you're just not giving me that. I just want you to know
that I love you, and I will always love you.
But, I just can't do this anymore.

✡ Let Down Again

Proem Genesis
All I've ever needed...
Girl, you already know...
"Do you want something like that?
Alright, I'm with it"

Bridge
Girl, I put it (my heart) on the line for you.
I keep wasting all of my time on you.
Why do I never get what I would do?
Can't you feel all of the pain I've been through?

Panorama
I came up; I didn't run. I was stuck,
get locked up, don't make bond – that's my luck.
She took me through it; I admit I lost my trust.
I gave it my all, but I guess it wasn't enough.

I'm all about that.
I'd never clout that.
Every time that she sent a text
I hit her right back.

Pan. III
Who would have thought I would like that?
I'd never type that.
How did it turn from a "nightcap"
to "Now I might like that?"

Hey, Look!
I'm hearing voices in my head, am I head I crazy?
Rewind time, Girl, I might make you my lady. Get you pregnant, Girl, we might just have a baby
You can be Queen B, I'll be your Jay-Z.

Pan. V
I'm getting there – *Yes.*
In your underwear on Facetime, Yes – I'm coming there to bring this thunder there – Yes.
I used to drive a Honda there and talk to you mama there.
If we're talking bands, I've got a hundred now
and that's on my mother.
Yes! Hey! Look!

Apogee / Act III
"Baby, I'm sorry. I don't know what I was thinking.
But, I promise, I promise, I promise I know you
probably have heard this before. And that's why you're
not picking up the phone, that's why you're not listening
to me, that's why you're believing me. But, I promise
if you give me one more shot, I'm going to make this better.
I promise".

Act VI

"Once again you have reached the one and only, that's all around. Leave me a detailed message and I will retrieve it. If you call with some B.S., I'm not going to answer. For someone calling restricted, In't going to answer. So to make a long story short, do not call my phone with any B.S., because I don't tolerate it. So with that being said, you have a blessed one."

Panorama
On the block, I might drop the top.
I don't play with ops.
Treat them like a Franck Muller,
Shhh, all I do is watch.

Hold up, hold up, hold up, hold up, hold up, hold up.

Pan. III
I'm about to come back at it from the jump a little different.

Money on my mind, money on my line;
I'm not lying. Why would I waste time?
I took my lick and I never dropped a dime.
Even when the sun's down,
I still shine – that's on slime.
I pray you don't try to slide;
They're outside.
There's too much money in these streets
But they don't see it, I guess they're blind.
I'm always working every day, Girl, we can't link I don't have time.
But, you're fine though.
Where'd they find you?
Girl, my chain costs a ticket I might blind you.
If it's whack when I hit it, I won't call you.

I told my dog to handle that, yes, that's dog food.
Let's make it clear, I get mine in lumps. I do not do fronts.
My pocket's on the Klumps.
I've got what you want, I'm on point.
She slapped her home-girl on the thigh and said, "I can't lie, girl, that's my joint."
Talking on the phone, she said that my voice makes her moist.
"But, I already knew that. So why would you go do that?
So, if you take it out and bend over I might run through that.
She got on top and rode it like a drop.
I told her "Don't stop."
I put her hand together from behind, I stroked it like a cop.

♆ An'im Zemirot תורימז םיענא

Dear Lord,

I would like to a close
by saying thank YOU.
I titled this project Old Testament
because of how far I've come.
The old me and the new me
are almost complete opposites of
one another; and those changes
for the better would not have been possible
without YOU. YOU were with me every
step of the way and when others did,
YOU never walked away.
YOU could have,
quite frankly YOU
should have;
but YOU didn't.
I appreciate it.

Honoring the Father, giving thanks
to the Son, and being guided by
the light of the Holy Spirit; in
Jesus' most Holy Name

I pray, Amen.
One /G\

Epistles from the Author

Death Certificate, in its penned and aural contour, is a dramatic monologue. A dramatic monologue is a poetic work whereby the speaker addresses the audience about a topic while unwittingly revealing details about him/herself. In this particular dramatic monologue, the speaker reveals how traumatic it was to lose his grandmother by letting the audience know a few of the many things she did for him prior to her passing. In doing so, he unwittingly reveals things to the audience that he would not have otherwise. This retrospectively centers the story he intends to tell behind the story he actually tells around the circumference of a phrase his grandmother often used – "You did this on yourself." Although this phrase is grammatically incorrect, it contains great spiritual substance. While addressing the audience, he often derails throughout the piece by addressing his grandmother directly, repeatedly asking her if she can hear him. This work expresses loss through the lenses of anger, love, and rage. In essence, the first line of panorama one seemingly serves as a foundation for the piece as a whole, when the speaker states "I put that on all of my partners". Of course to "put something on someone" is a voodoo term meaning to "curse," however as the text unfolds we find that the partners to whom the speaker refers are merely personifications created by his multifaceted ego that often fails to distinguish reality from illusory.

No Ingés // Act I, in its penned and aural contour, is a cacophony. A cacophony poem is a poetic work written using an array of clashing consonants. For this reason, when spoken aloud these poems are usually difficult to recite and typically unpleasant to the ear. One of the most well-known cacophony poems is Lewis Carroll's "Jabberwocky." The reason that this particular poem was written as a cacophony is to illustrate the lingual disconnect between the speaker and his beloved.

Confirmation, in its penned and aural contour, is a burlesque. A burlesque is a poem, play, or story that simplifies an otherwise serious subject by presenting it in a ludicrous or trivial manner. The word burlesque derives from the Italian word *burla,* which means to make light of through ridicule or mockery. In *Confirmation,* the speaker mocks a woman's longing for the man to "confirm" that he loves her according to seemingly superficial standards, at least from his perspective, despite confirming so financially. Although men, by their very nature, are providers; they only provide for those that they love – thus when a man truly loves a woman, his love for her will reflect in what he does for her monetarily. The poem opens with a proem genesis that shifts back and forth from passive voice to present voice. This is intentionally done to reflect how blurry the line between love and hate can become in an unstable relationships. Oftentimes, the people in the relationship have difficulties understanding if they are building a stronger bond or simply going through the motions. This is the reason the word 'complicated' has grown in recent years as a term to categorize relationships, and in some cases even marriages. And, it is that very sort of complication that the speaker highlights while still attempting to make the woman he loves to feel secure.

D4L, regarding its penned and aural contour, is a response poem. A response poem is written to answer a question addressed to the speaker. Although, the person that initially asked the question is generally not included in the piece, in most response poems the speaker paraphrases the question toward the end of the composition to provide perspective. In this particular response poem, the speaker addresses the question, "What are you looking for in a woman?" Just as *Confirmation* shifts from passive voice to present voice, so does this piece. In D4L, however, it is intentionally done so to reflect how the things that we want now and what we wanted in the past can change yet essentially remain the same.

Roses Are Red // Act II, regarding its penned and aural contour, is an ekphrastic poem. Within the aural contour, *The Corpus Hermeticum* was cited. An ekphrastic derives from the Greek word for "description." In this particular poem, the speaker seems to have found the love of his life; or has he? The answer to that very question is something not specified within the penned or aural contour to purposely force the audience to form their own opinion and conclusion.

Let Down Again // Act III, in its penned and aural contour, is a downtrodden poem. A downtrodden poem is a poetic work that expresses great oppression. The oppression could be to a substance, a situation, or even to a person. This particular downtrodden poem is the speaker's attempt to explain the things that have subjugated him in efforts to educate the audience to the fact that no problem is greater than the person going through it.

Come Correct // Act IV, regarding its penned and aural contour, is a satirical interval. A satirical interval is an inflated illustration of humor. In this particular satirical interval, upon completion of his book, the One/G\'s calls his publishing company to submit materials. After mistakenly dialing the wrong number, he finds himself listening to one of the most bizarre voicemail greetings that he has probably ever heard.

Credentials

Following street code, I would like to send a special thanks to all those that have contributed
to this project without including any names.
You all know who you are.
Thank You.
Shalom.

Z7

Printed in the United States
By Bookmasters